Dress Up One Direction

Illustrated by Georgie Fearns

Edited by Jen Wainwright
Designed by Zoe Bradley

D1376844

Buster Books

Contents

I ♡ LIAM

Mrs Styles!

I Love Louis x

True Directioner

Niall 4 Eva

It's Time To Dress Up One Direction

There's no doubt about it,
One Direction is the hottest boy band on the
planet! Now's your chance to become the boys'
stylist, and make sure Louis, Zayn, Harry, Liam
and Niall always look their gorgeous best.

With over 350 glossy stickers, you can dress the 1D
lads in their signature styles, or mix and match the
clothes to come up with your own
unique looks. There are even some extra stickers
that you can use to decorate stuff.

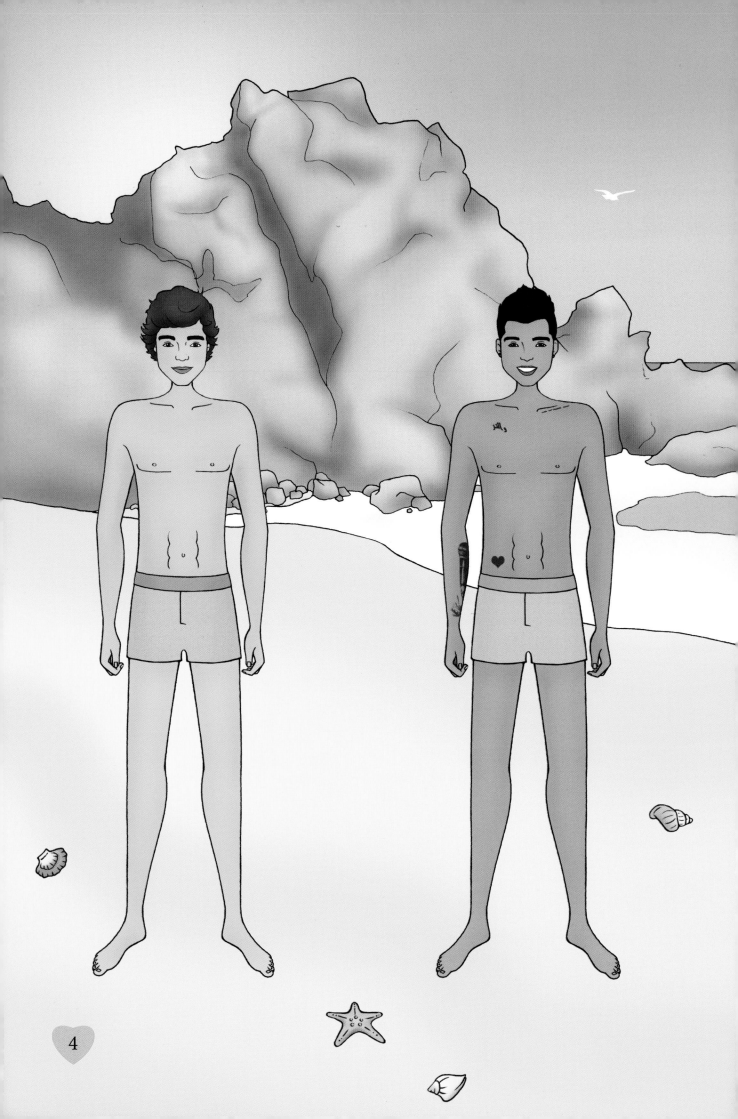

What Makes You Beautiful

The boys are wrapping up their video shoot on the beach in California. There's been lots of fun in the sun, and Louis has even had a run-in with the police for driving a camper van too slowly. Oops!

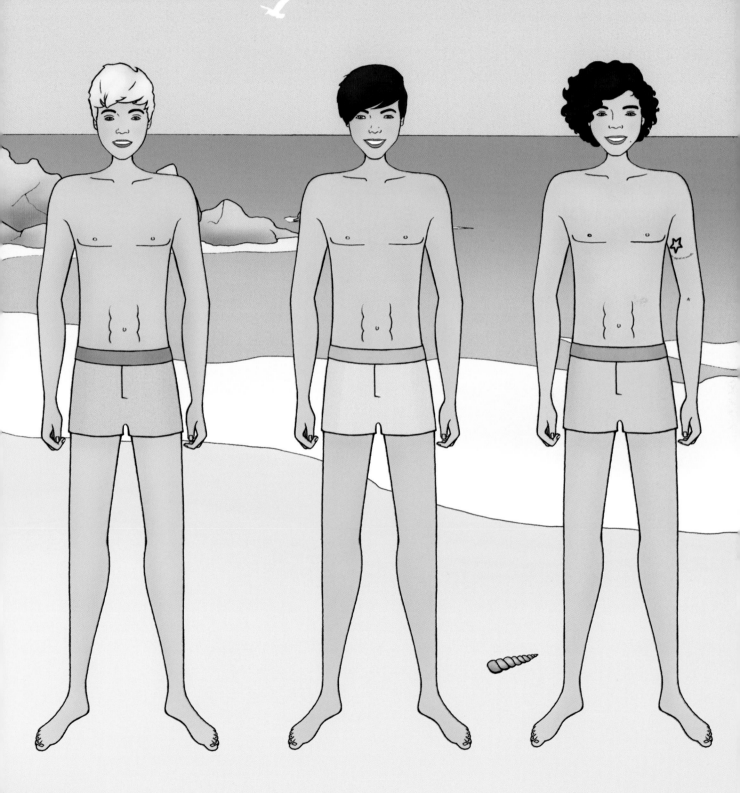

It's Gotta Be You

The romantic video for 1D's second smash-hit single is being filmed at Lake Placid in upstate New York, and poor Liam is scared there'll be crocodiles lurking in the lake. Nights by the lakeside can get pretty chilly, even with a roaring campfire, so the lads need to wrap up warm and look stylish.

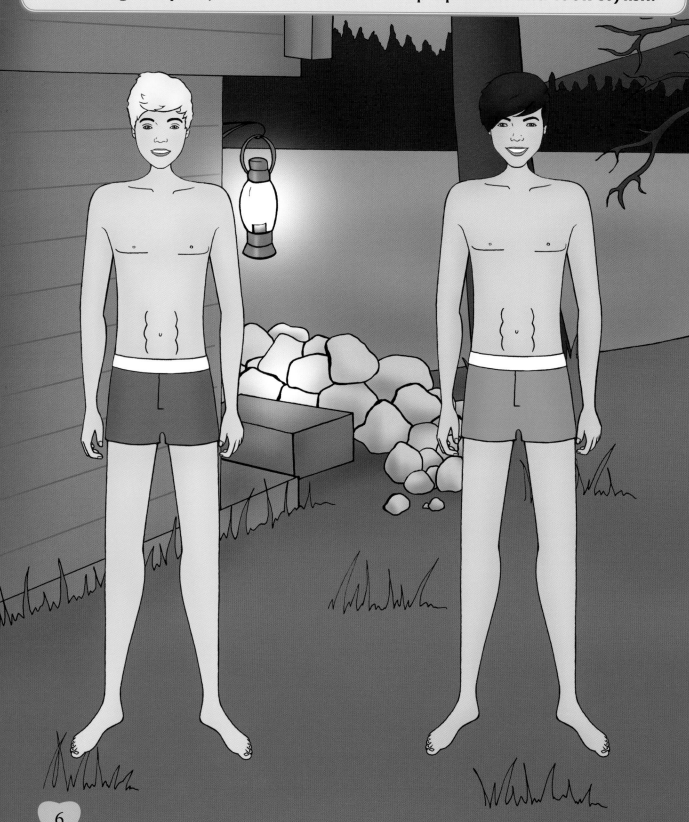

6

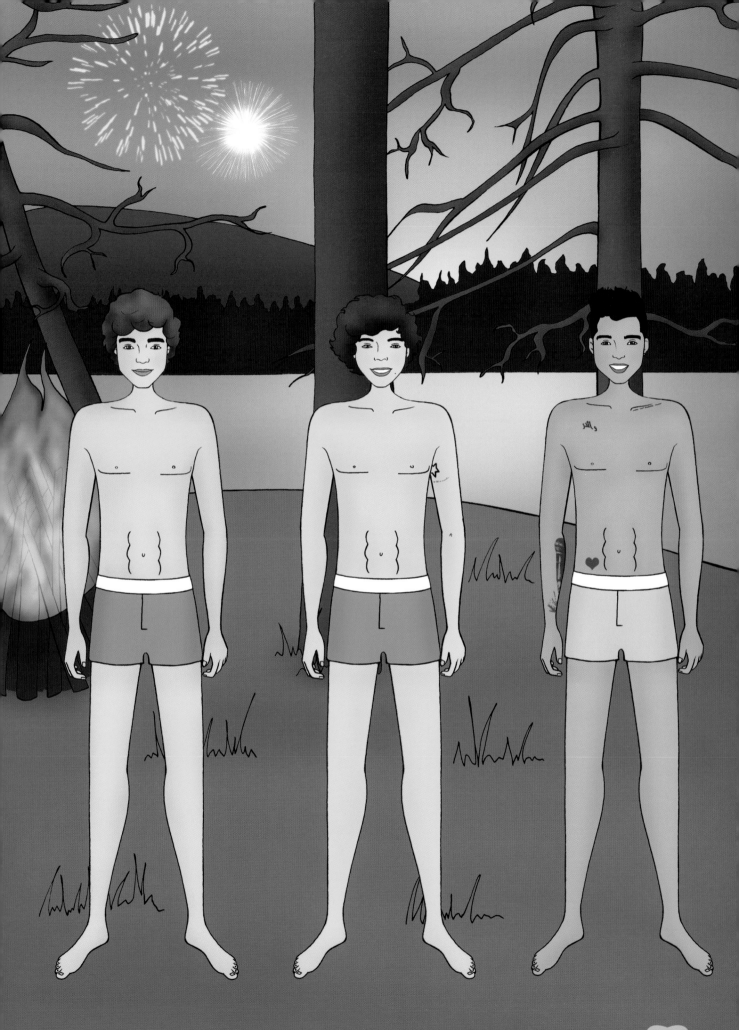

You've Got That One Thing

The boys have got a busy day planned shooting their new video on location in London. There's lots of fun ahead in Battersea Park, Trafalgar Square and Covent Garden, so dress them up to look their best.

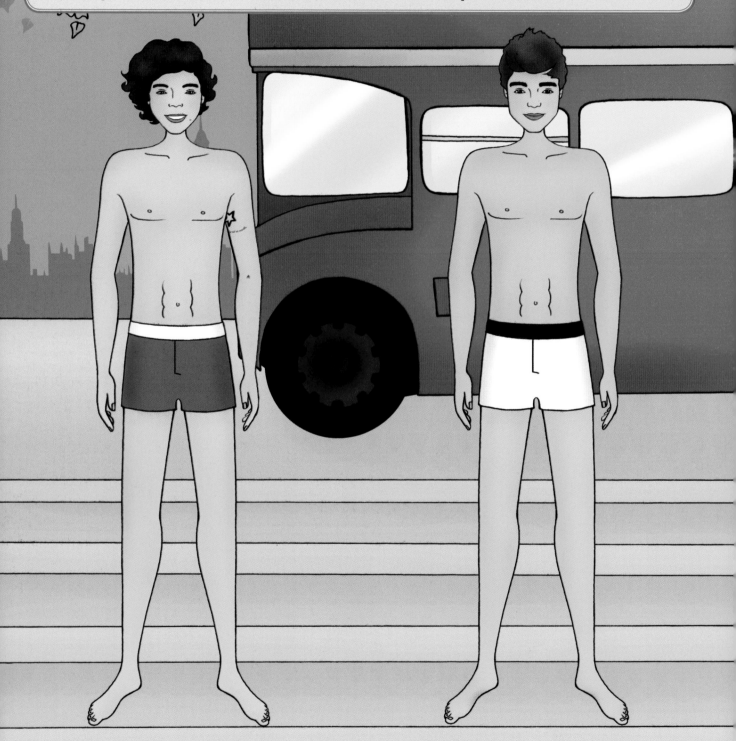

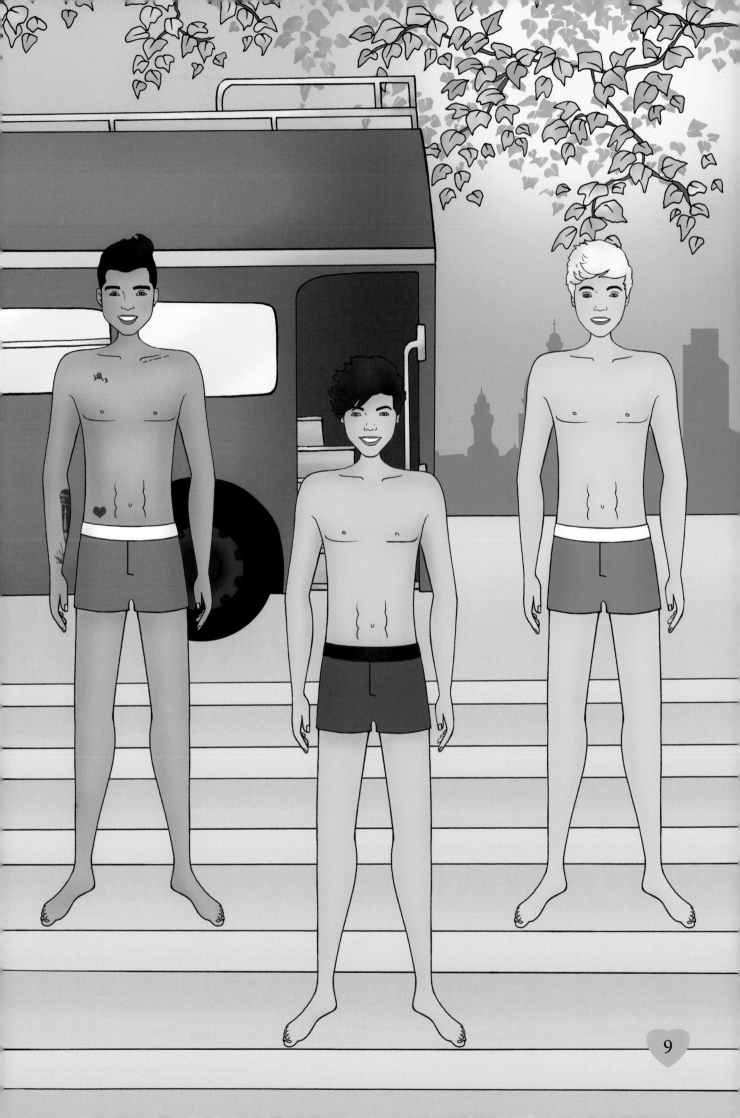

The Camera Loves Them

It's time for a photoshoot and One Direction are in high spirits.
Dress them in bright clothes to match their mood.

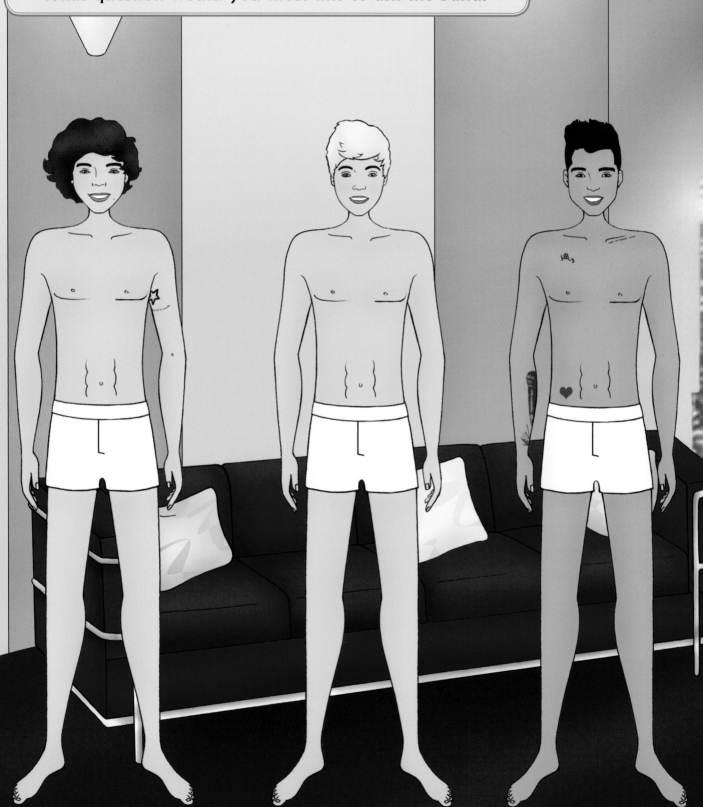

An Exclusive Interview

Everyone wants to know what makes the 1D boys tick, and this primetime interview might just reveal some secrets. What question would you most like to ask the band?

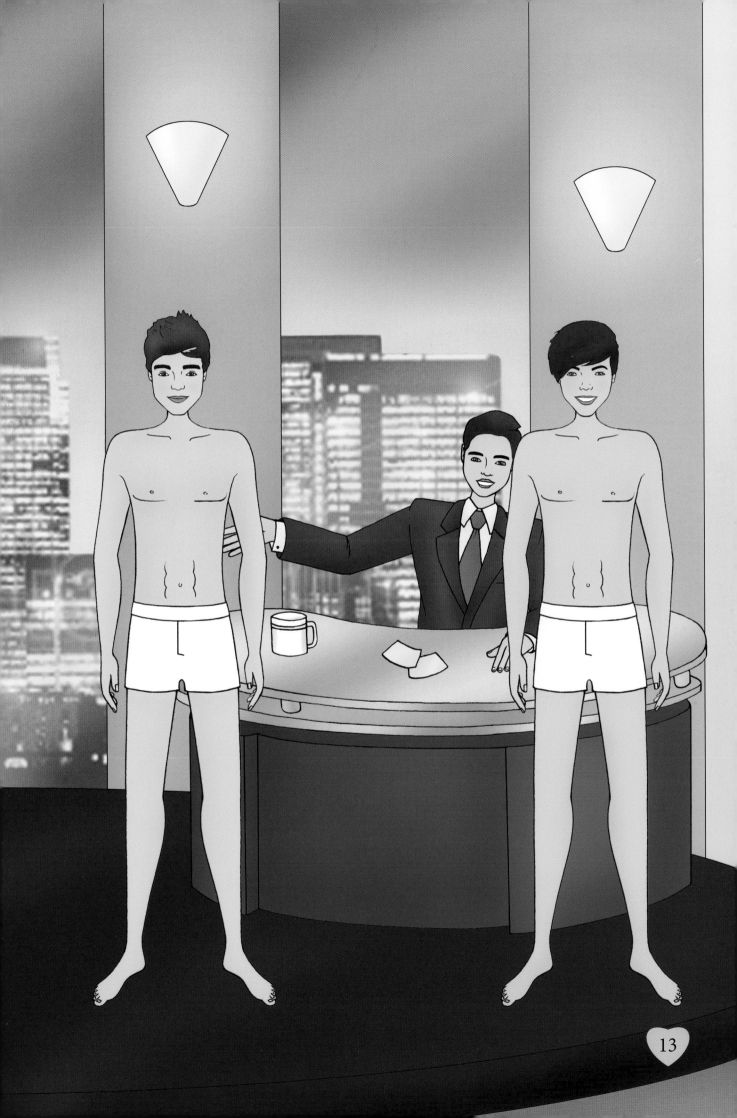

At The Brits

It's time to hit the red carpet at The Brit Awards. The boys need to be dressed in their sharpest suits, as by the end of the night they'll be walking away with the award for Best British Single. Woohoo!

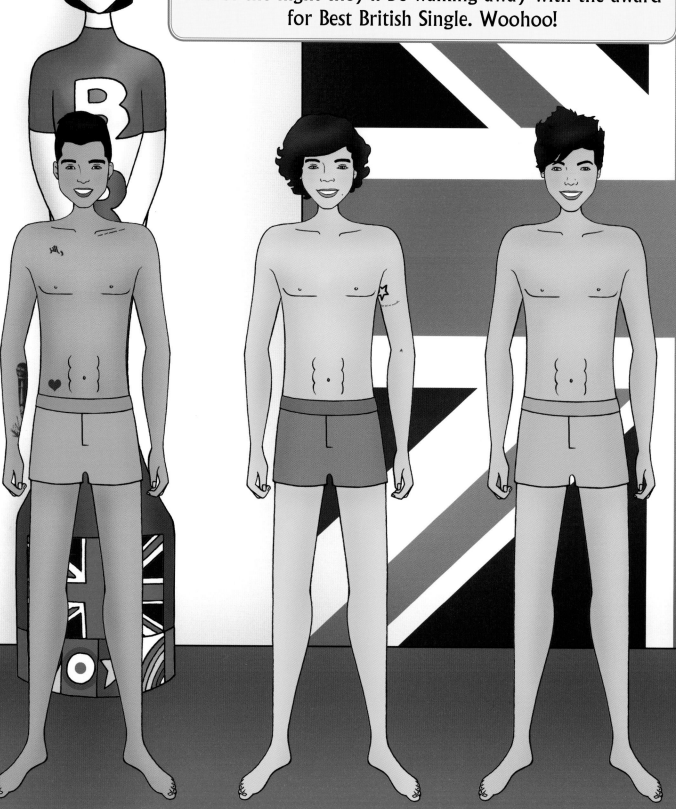

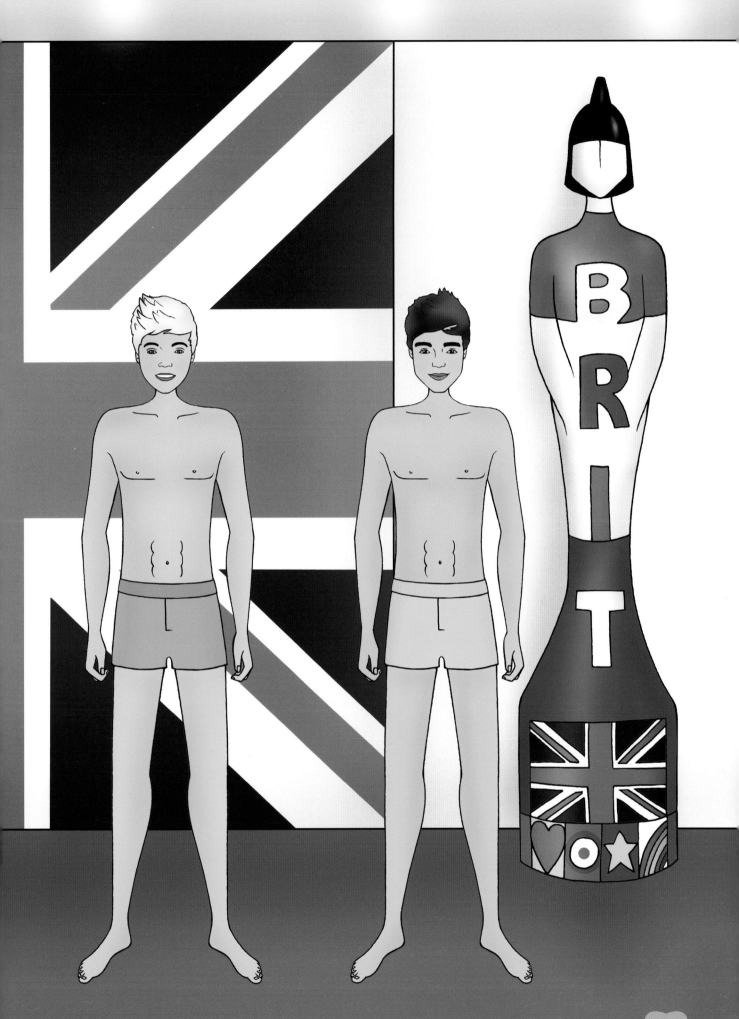

Show Time!

The arena is jam-packed with Directioners who can't wait to
see their dream boys take to the stage. Make sure the lads are
looking stylish so they can take the crowd by storm.

Theme Park Fun

The hardworking lads are taking a well-deserved day off for some fun at the theme park. With white-knuckle rides galore to enjoy, which one of the boys will scream the loudest?

The Olympic Closing Ceremony

It's a huge deal for the One Direction boys to be playing at the closing ceremony for the Olympic Games. The whole world is watching, so make sure they're all suitably dressed.

It's A Hat Trick

To win one award at the MTV Video Music Awards would be a real achievement, but those amazing One Direction boys have won three! Dress them in slick suits so they can bask in the glory.

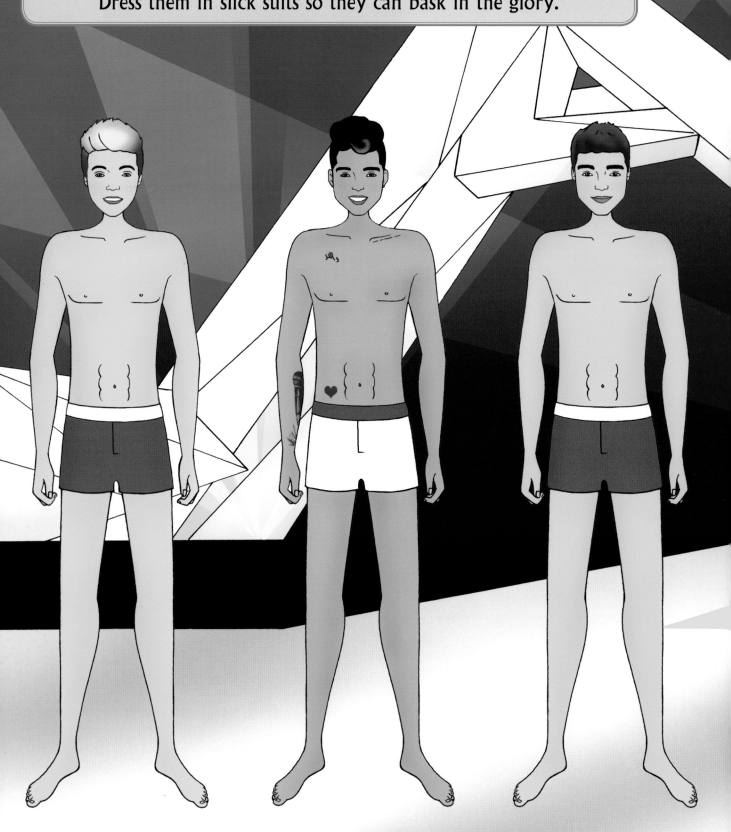

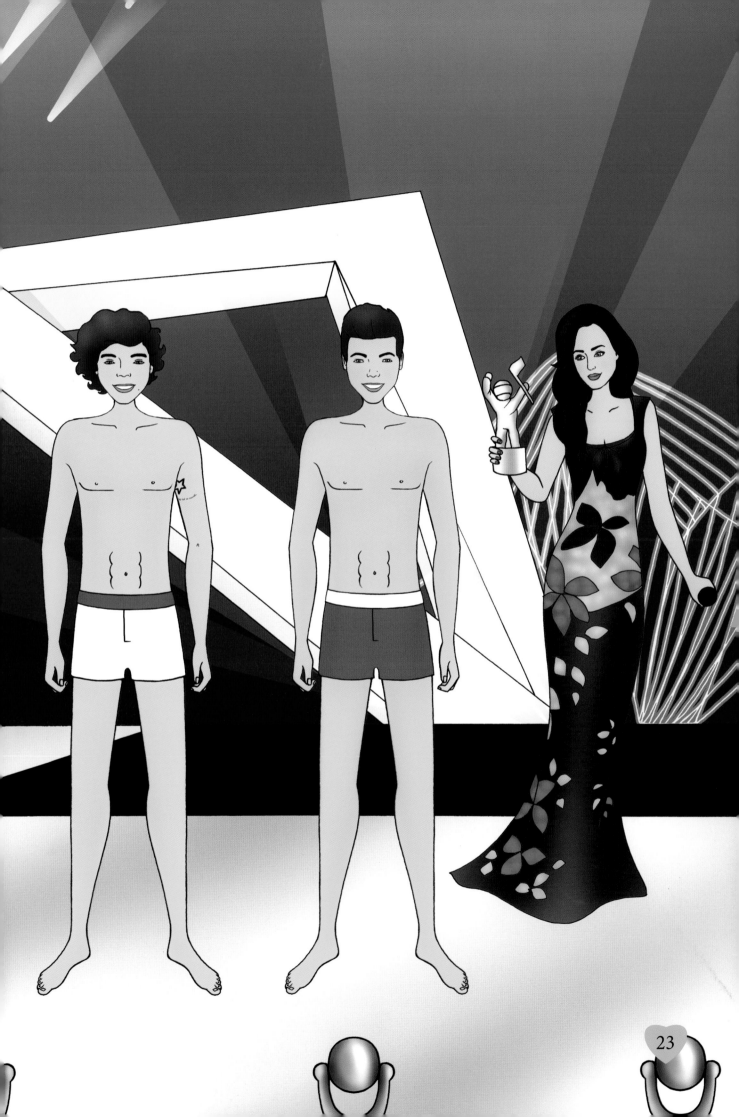

Add heart and star stickers to this One Direction scrapbook page to show that you're a true super fan.

For Eleanor Bryant

First published in Great Britain in 2013 by Buster Books, an imprint of Michael O'Mara Books Limited, 9 Lion Yard, Tremadoc Road, London SW4 7NQ

www.busterbooks.co.uk

Copyright © 2013 Buster Books

All rights reserved. No part of this publication may be reproduced, stored in a retrieval system, or transmitted in any form or by any means, electronic, mechanical, photocopying, recording or otherwise, without prior permission of the publisher.

ISBN: 978-1-78055-162-3

2 4 6 8 10 9 7 5 3 1

This book was printed in February 2013 by Ruho Corporation Sdn. Bhd., 334 Sungai Puyu, 13020 Butterworth, Penang, Malaysia.

Pages 4 – 5

Pages 6 – 7

Pages 12 – 13

Pages 14 – 15

Pages 16 – 17

Mrs Horan

Mrs Tomlinson

Mrs Malik

Mrs Payne

**Mrs Styles

Harry makes me happy

Louis is lovely

Pages 18 – 19

No-one's like Niall

*AmaZayn

Liam is lush

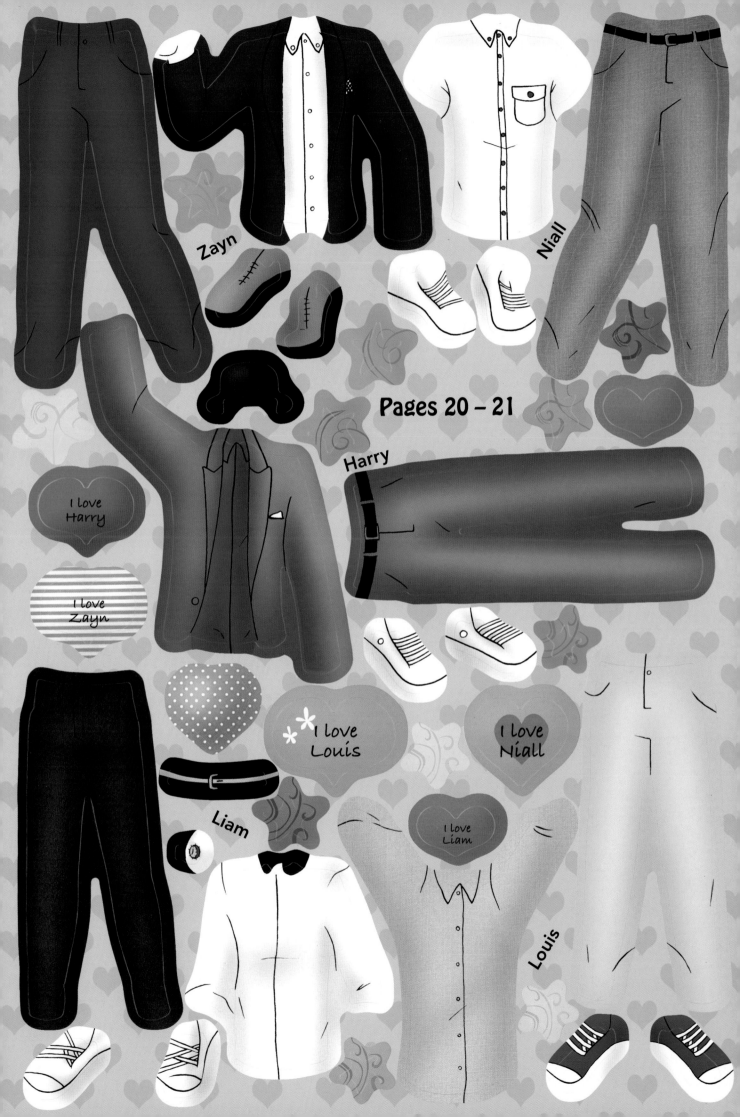

Zayn

Niall

Pages 20 – 21

Harry

I love Harry

I love Zayn

I love Louis

I love Niall

Liam

I love Liam

Louis